c o n t e n t s

introduction

t is tempting to say that in a truly loving relationship, there should be no rigid demarcation between the preliminaries to sex and the culmination of the act. Yet this view is often voiced by individuals – women as well as men – who rush through or skip the tempting early dishes that can form an essential part of the whole, in order to hog the main course. At the other extreme, foreplay can become an obsession in itself, leading a partner to complain: 'I wish he (or she) would get on with it'! With these two extremes in mind, it is the aim of this 'pillow book', *Sexual Foreplay*, to place the preliminaries of sex firmly in the context of the total enjoyment of a sexual relationship.

The preliminaries to sex can play an important part in aligning the slightly different rates of arousal in men and women. Although these are hardly noticeable as a rule, they are surprisingly often the root cause of sexual maladjustment between a couple. In our culture men really do turn on more quickly than women. However, not everyone can enjoy sex on a 'wham, bam, thank you ma'am!' basis, and if you do really want to please a woman on an equal basis, you must take the trouble to ensure that she is as ready as you to reach peak enjoyment.

This is not to suggest that foreplay is solely the duty of the man, or indeed a duty at all . . . an impression widely canvassed by non-playing coaches, but very far from the truth. Foreplay can, and should, be enormous fun in its own right, provided it does not become an obsession and leave you and your partner stuck forever in first gear. All the interchanges of lovers — before, during and after sex — are joyful, and in the act of love all these interchanges should merge into one another. If you enjoy love, you will naturally act together to give and receive the maximum pleasure, holding back or pressing forward as need may be.

So read on from here . . . and go at the speed that suits you both best!

Alex Comfort M.B.,D.Sc.

love

We use the same word for man–woman, mother–child, child–parent, and I–mankind relations – rightly, because they are a continuous spectrum. In talking about sexual relations, it seems right to apply it to any relationship in which there is mutual tenderness, respect and consideration – from a total interdependence where the death of one maims the other for years, to an agreeable night together. The intergrades are all love, all worthy, all part of human experience.

Some meet the needs of one person, some of another – or of the same person at different times. That's really the big problem of sexual ethics, and it's basically a problem of self-understanding and of communication. You can't assume that your 'conditions of love' are applicable to, or accepted by, any other party; you can't assume that these won't be changed quite unpredictably in both of you by the experience of loving; you can't necessarily know your own mind.

love . . . *the essential openness of a real relationship between people* . . .

f sexual love can be – and it is – the supreme human experience, it must be also a bit hazardous. It can give us our best and our worst moments. In this respect it's like mountain climbing – over-timid people miss the whole experience; reasonably balanced and hardy people accept the risks for the rewards, but realize that there's a difference between this and being foolhardy. Love, moreover, involves someone else's neck beside your own. At least you can make as sure as may be that you don't exploit or injure someone. Getting them to sign a form of consent before they start isn't the answer either. There was a hell of a lot to be said for the English Victorian idea of not being a cad ('person devoid of finer or gentlemanly feelings'). A cad can be of either sex.

Marriage between two rival actor-managers, each trying to produce the other regardless, isn't love. The relationship between a prostitute and a casual client where, for reasons they don't quite get, real tenderness and respect occur, is.

love *A potentially overwhelming experience*
worth all the risks

t e n d e r n e s s

enderness doesn't exclude extremely violent games (though many people neither need nor want these), but it does exclude clumsiness, heavy handedness, lack of feedback, spitefulness and non-rapport generally, shown fully in the way you touch each other. What it implies at root is a constant awareness of what your partner is feeling, plus the knowledge of how to heighten that feeling, gently, toughly, slowly or fast, and this only comes from an inner state of mind between you. No really tender person can just turn over and go to sleep.

Many if not most inexperienced men, and some women, are just naturally clumsy – either through haste, through anxiety, or through lack of sensing how the other sex feels. Men in general are harder-skinned than women – don't grab breasts, stick fingers

tenderness *What it implies is a constant awareness*
of what your partner is feeling

tenderness *Gently does it*
can be exciting for both of you

into the vagina, handle female skin as if it was your own, or (and this goes for both sexes) misplace bony parts of your anatomy. More girls respond to very light than to very heavy stimulation – just brushing pubic hair or skin hairs will usually do far more than a whole-hand grab. At the same time don't be frightened – neither of you is made of glass. Women by contrast often fail to use enough pressure, especially in handwork, though the light, light variety is a sensation on its own. Start very gently, making full use of the skin surface, and work up. Stimulus toleration in any case increases with sexual excitement until even hard blows can become excitants (though not for everyone). This loss of pain sense disappears almost instantly with orgasm, so don't go on too long, and be extra gentle as soon as he or she has come.

If you are really heavy-handed, a little practice with inanimate surfaces, dress-fastenings and so on will help. Male strength is a turn-on in sex, but it isn't expressed in clumsy handwork, bear-hugs and brute force – at least not as starters. If there is a problem here, remember you both can talk. Few people want to be in bed on any terms with a person who isn't basically tender, and most people are delighted to be in bed with the right person who is. The ultimate test is whether you can bear to find the person there when you wake up. If you are actually pleased, then you're onto the right thing.

f i d e l i t y

idelity, infidelity, jealousy and so on. We've deliberately not gone into the ethics of lifestyle. The facts are that few men and slightly more women in our culture go through life with sexual experience confined to one partner only. What suits a particular couple depends on their needs, situation, anxieties and so on. These needs are a particularly delicate problem in communication: if mutual comprehension is complete and ongoing you can count yourselves lucky. Active deception always hurts a relationship. Complete frankness which is aimed to avoid guilt or as an act of aggression against a partner can do the same. The real problem arises from the fact that sexual relations can be anything, for different people and on different occasions, from a game to a total fusion of identities; the heartaches arise when

fidelity *In a relationship this means that you know where each of you stands*

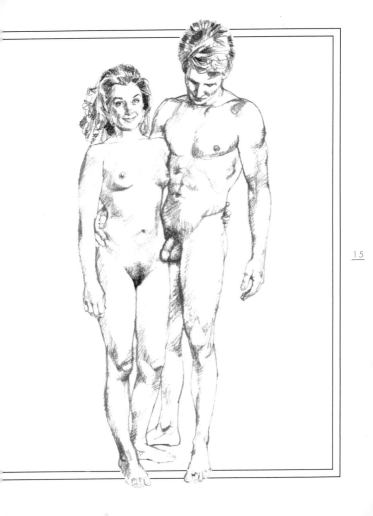

each partner sees it differently. There is no sexual relationship which doesn't involve responsibility, because there are two or more people involved: anything which, as it were, militantly excludes a partner is hurtful, yet to be whole people we have at some point to avoid total fusion with each other – 'I am I and you are you, and neither of us is on earth to live up to the other's expectations.' People who communicate sexually have to find their own fidelities. All we can suggest is that you discuss them so that at least you know where each of you stands.

fidelity *All relationships involve responsibility to yourself and to each other*

real sex

he sort our culture and most admass propaganda don't recognize: not that intercourse or masturbation or genital kisses aren't real sex, but some other things are real sex too, which people need, but which don't excite our time and age. We can list some: being together in a situation of pleasure, or of danger, or just of rest (if we admitted these as sexual we'd run the risk of having to love other people as people, and that would be worrying or inconvenient, to us or society); touching; old fashioned expedients like holding hands; sleeping together even without, or especially after, intercourse.

Most women don't need telling this, but are as shy about telling it to males, for fear of seeming sentimental, as males are about object-preferences or aggressive needs.

real sex *Tenderness, touching and being together*
are as much 'real sex' as vaginal intercourse

f o o d

*D*inner is a traditional preface to sex. In old-time France or Austria one booked a restaurant room with no handle on the outside. A meal *à deux* is a direct lead-in but don't include alcohol: it's a powerful neutering drug, and is the commonest cause of unexpected impotence. Some people enjoy food-and-sex games (custard or icecream on the skin, grapes in the pussy) but these can be messy for a domestic setting. Most lovers with privacy like to eat naked together and take it from there.

History is littered with 'aphrodisiac' foods – magic (eryngo roots, which look like testicles, phallic asparagus and so on), olfactory (fish, fresh-picked tomatoes straight off the plant which smell sexy) or miscellaneous. One can't prove that onions, eels – phallic or otherwise – ginseng and so on don't work on some people. Any reputed aphrodisiac works if you think it will, while many pharmacological responses can get overridden in individuals by other factors. Broad beans are a reputed aphrodisiac – not only

food *Eating naked together is better than any aphrodisiac*

do they look like testicles, but they contain dopamine. Hot spices, which induce skin flushing, are another plausible line of attack.

But no alleged aphrodisiac is a lifesaver, or comes up to the effect of 'the time and the place and the loved one together' However, experiment by all means. Only heavy meals and excessive drinking are specific turnoffs and need to be avoided.

dancing

All ballroom dancing in pairs looks towards inter-course. In this respect the Puritans were dead right. The development of no-contact dances has come about because one doesn't now need a social excuse to embrace a girl, but as an excitant it need not involve contact at all – in fact dances like the flamenco or the twist are far more erotic than a clinch because you aren't too close to see one another. At its best this sort of dance is simply intercourse by remote control (see pages 36-37).

Most good lovers dance well together. They can do it publicly or in private, clothed or naked. Stripping one another while dancing is a sensation on its own. Don't hurry to full intercourse – dance until his erection is unbearable and she is almost coming, brought there by rhythm and the sight and perfume of each other alone. Even then you need not stop.

dancing *At its best, dancing is simply intercourse by remote control*

Most couples can insert and continue dancing, either in each other's arms, or limbo-style, linked only by the penis, provided they are the right heights. Unfortunately this means that the woman needs to be at least as tall as the man, while as a rule she's going to be shorter. Otherwise he has to bend his knees, which is tiring. If you can't dance inserted, and she is small, pick her up into one of the Hindu standing positions, legs round waist, arms round neck, and continue like this. If she is too heavy to pick up, turn her and take her stooping from behind, still keeping the dance going.

Seduction, or encouragement, while dancing is a natural. In the days of formal dancing one used to wish that the girl had her breasts on her back, where one could reach them, but that would have made it too easy. Gentle pressure, rhythm, sight and scent, and a knowledge of remote-control methods are all that is needed to bring the dance on to its erotic conclusion.

dancing *Seduction, or encouragement,*
while dancing is a natural

handwork

ex for all males and many females begins in the handwork class – when we start to discover our own bodies and when we start to have access to each other's. For both sexes it is basic training – in mutual sex good handwork is never superseded. A couple who can masturbate each other skillfully can do anything else they like, and a generation brought up to masturbate with enjoyment from pre-adolescence will have a flying start in forming some sensual attitudes. Handwork is not a 'substitute' for vaginal intercourse but quite different, giving a different type of orgasm, and the orgasm one induces oneself is different again from the orgasm induced by a partner. In full intercourse it is a preparation – to stiffen him, or to give her one or more preliminary peaks before insertion. After intercourse, it is the natural lead-in to a further round. Moreover most men can get a second orgasm sooner from partner-stimulation than from the vagina, and a third after that if they masturbate themselves.

slow masturbation
*This is a mind-blowing
way of prolonging sex
for both of you*

A *woman* who has

the divine gift of lechery

and loves her partner will masturbate

him well, and a woman who knows how to masturbate a man –

subtly, unhurriedly and mercilessly – will almost always make a

superlative partner. She needs intuitive empathy and real

enjoyment of a penis, holding it in just the right place, with just the

right amount of pressure and movement, and timing her action in

bursts to coincide with his feeling – stopping or slowing to keep him in suspense, speeding up to control his climax. Some men can't stand really proficient masturbation to climax unless they are securely tied, and virtually none can hold still for slow masturbation.

The variation can be endless, even if she hasn't the choice of foreskin back, foreskin not back, which again yield two quite distinct nuances. If he isn't circumcised she will probably need to avoid rubbing the glans itself, except in pursuit of very special effects. Her best grip is just below the groove, with the skin back as far as it will go, and using two hands – one pressing hard near the root, holding the penis steady, or fondling the scrotum, the other making a thumb-and-first finger ring, or a whole hand grip. She should vary this, and, in prolonged masturbation, change hands often. For a full orgasm she sits comfortably on his chest or kneels astride him. During every extended sexual session one orgasm – usually the second or third – is well worth giving in this way: the French professionals who used no other method and called themselves *'les filles de la Poignet'* didn't only stay in business through fear of infection. It is well worth devoting time to perfecting this technique – it fully expresses love and can be domesticated in any bedroom.

pattes d'araignée
exotic massage at its most delicate

Rolling the penis like pastry between the palms of two hands is another technique, best used for producing an erection rather than going for orgasm. Firm pressure with one finger at the midpoint between penis and anus is another. For some occasions she can try to copy his own favourite method of self-masturbation. When she uses her own rhythm it has a different and sometimes more startling effect.

He needs to notice how she masturbates herself. Clitoral rubbing can be as mind-blowing for her as slow masturbation is for him, but it can be painful if it is unskillful, repeated too often or straight after an orgasm achieved in this way. She says: 'The main difficulty from the man's point of view is that the ideal pressure point varies from hour to hour so he should allow her to guide him in the right place. Most men think they know automatically, having succeeded once – they are often wrong.'

For preparation as well as orgasm, the flat of the hand on the vulva with the middle finger between the lips, and its tip moving in and out of the vagina, while the ball of the palm presses hard just above the pubis, is probably the best method. Steady rhythm is the most important thing, taking it from her hip move-

handwork *Try copying his favourite method of self-masturbation*

ments, and alternating with gentle lip stretching – then a full attack on the clitoris and its hood with the forefinger or little finger, thumb deeply in the vagina (keep your nails short). For faster response, hold her open with one hand and work gently with all the fingers of the other (in this case she may need to be fixed down). Switch to the tongue if she becomes dry, because she won't realize until afterwards how sore you have made her.

In mutual masturbation to orgasm you take out your need to move on your partner. It works better than *soixante-neuf* because you can let go without losing your partner or hurting them. Side by side on your backs is probably the best position.

handwork *Once you've found a stimulus which makes you feel good, incorporate it into lovemaking and use it to the full*

When she masturbates him, she may get extra pleasure from seeing his ejaculation – if you want to avoid spilling semen in a strange bed, use one of the short glanscondoms called American tips (this is their only use – they are dangerous contraceptives, as they come off during intercourse).

However much sex you have, you will still need simple, own-hand masturbation – not only during periods of separation, but simply when you feel like having another orgasm. Some women feel left out if they find their partner masturbating; but if you feel vibrations when he thinks you are asleep and want to get in on the act, tackle him there and then and finish him yourself at full speed or

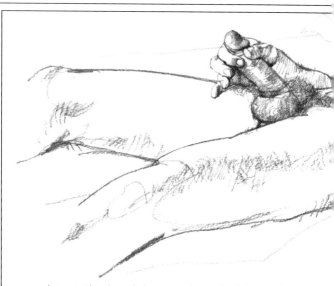

better, start him slow-style then stop, tie him, and make him watch you masturbate yourself, slowly and with style, before you put him out of his misery. The unexpected sight of a woman giving herself an orgasm when he cannot move is unbearably exciting for most men. Make sure he can't get loose. Finally, watching each other take the last orgasm separately but together makes a wonderful end to any afternoon in bed.

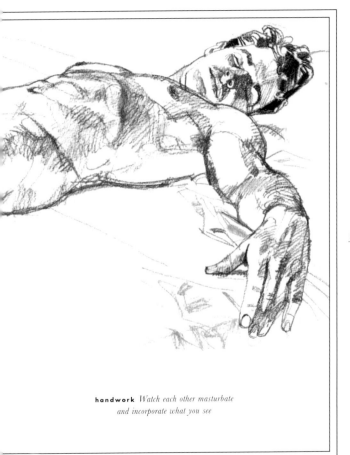

handwork *Watch each other masturbate
and incorporate what you see*

r e m o t e *c o n t r o l*

t is an old story that you can seduce a complete novice, who has no idea what you mean, by slipping a thumb into a closed fist, or between your lips, and absent mindedly moving it in and out, in and out. We'd like to see this. All of the people we have seen it work on have known very well what it was all about.

This is one version of the *pompido telecommando*. The lip one works better, nail downwards in the appropriate rhythm – she will feel it where she should. She can do the same 'at' him, for example eating. Once habituated to either of these tele-control devices, most girls and some men can be radio-controlled as to excitement, erection and even orgasm – even by rubbing the lobes of one's ear – from several places down a table, the opposite side of a room, or the opposite box at a theater. The funniest use we've seen of this was when the lady was dancing with

remote control *Private remote signals can wind you up to fever pitch*

someone else, who spotted what was going on in his arms but thought he was the source of the signals – which actually came from her lover, who was sitting out.

The original *telecommando* is the 'blower' which connects the restaurant with the kitchen downstairs. Appropriate.

friction rub

The original meaning of shampoo, which is gentle kneading massage all over. Much more pleasant if you shed all adult inhibitions and rub each other all over with one of the non-messy

friction rub *Soaping one another all over leads on naturally to better things*

scented lotions one can buy now for the purpose – a perfumery gimmick that shows a lot more insight than flavoured douches and so on. Sit on something that doesn't matter and rub each other, together or in turns – sunburn oil or soap lather work well if you haven't got a special preparation.

This always ends in genital handwork, then intercourse, then bath together. Semen would be the ideal medium, but it is too little and too late – bottle lotion is a substitute for this particular fantasy. She kneads his muscles, with fingers and a vibrator as well if they like; he concentrates on her breasts, buttocks, loins and neck. With practice these sensations are well worth cultivating. The Los Angeles massage parlors may get busted regularly, but they have nothing one can't do at home – apart from the fact that they are male-orientated, not mutual, and lay on a whole troupe of girls for every man.

mouth music

t is only a few decades ago that genital kisses, or rather the taboos on them, were a king pretext for divorce on grounds of perversity, cruelty and so on. We've come some way since then – now there are textbooks, and they figure in the movies.

Soixante-neuf is fine but has some drawbacks. It needs attention and care to give your partner your best, and consequently you can't go berserk over it, as you can over a mutual genital orgasm: impending orgasm, especially in the woman, just isn't compatible with careful technique, and the man can even be bitten. Another defect is that in *soixante-neuf* the woman is the wrong way around for tongue work on the most sensitive surface of the glans. Mutual kisses are wonderful, but if you are going to orgasm it's usually better to take turns.

mouth music *A spontaneous genital kiss to a man is one of the most moving gestures in the whole sexual experience*

*S*ome girls *do* and some don't like the man to go all the way and ejaculate. Those who don't can easily stop just short of getting him there and shift to another foyer such as between the breasts. Others once they are used to it don't find the experience complete unless their lover does ejaculate.

Normal genital odor is a big part of the genital kiss for both partners, which means that the parties should wash often, but not immediately beforehand: they ought to know each other well enough to say, if it is ever disagreeable, and switch or wait. A few minutes' vigorous intercourse will often put this right, though the woman's odor changes in character. Contraceptives can upset it too. The marketers of intimate deodorants and flavoured vaginal juices show evidence only of sexual inexperience. The woman's cassolette is her secret weapon. Some men respond violently to it without realizing the fact. His, by contrast, will please her more the longer she loves him. Wash with white soap, and here as everywhere treat deodorants the way a chef would treat deflavorants.

For some couples the simultaneous, *soixante-neuf*-type mutual kiss really does represent the ultimate in sensation. For them, since loss of control will be complete, the woman can't be

navel *To kiss or touch with, even, possibilities of intercourse*

43

the berserk type, nor want him to stop short of ejaculating. The woman-on-top position shown in most books is all right, especially if she combines mouth with handwork, but it gives the man a stiff neck. We favor the no-cushions position, ie head to tail on their sides, each with the under thigh drawn up as a cushion for the partner's head. The man can open her widely by slipping his arm in the crook of her upper knee.

The mutual kiss can be long or short; the short is just in
passing – the long can last minutes or hours according to taste
and speed. Both fit nicely between rounds of intercourse, as well
as acting as hors d'oeuvres or a corpse reviver.

If, on the other hand, they are going alternately, let him start,
preferably in this same no-cushions position,
while she does very little.

mouth music *One can give the woman dozens of orgasms in
this way and she may still want to go on from there*

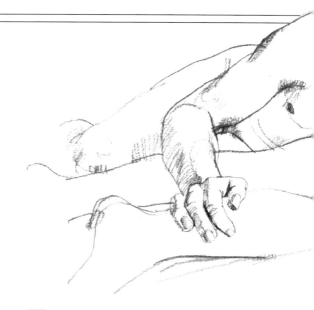

Then it can be her turn; or they can go on to intercourse, putting off fellatio until he has had one orgasm and a rest and is due for his next erection. In this way she can abandon herself, and watch her technique when she sucks him. Her technique depends on the man – for instance, on whether or not he is circumcised. Not all men find tongue or lip contact with the glans

tongue bath
Slow, all-over arousal

pleasurable. For some it's ecstasy, while others prefer foreskin movement over the glans with the shaft held tight. For a more active male position and a fast orgasm, she lies back, and he has oral coitus as fully and deeply as she can stand it. She must keep her teeth open, making him a vagina with her lips and tongue. He should keep control, to avoid being involuntarily bitten.

The reverse equivalent is when she kneels astride and gives herself, exactly as in a passionate mouth-to-mouth kiss, brushing first, then open and deeply, while he uses long tongue strokes from the vagina to the clitoris, with an extra twitch to her glans as he reaches it each time.

When it's his initiative, he can do worse than try the cascade position, if she is portable. This is really only *soixante-neuf* standing up, but it gives her the unique sensation of an orgasm head-downward. To get her there he lays her face-up across the bed, head over the edge, stands astride her face, then bends over and picks her up, legs round his neck. She can return his kiss, but near orgasm she had far better slip him between her breasts or into her hand, and abandon herself to full orgasm.

In the other direction good mouthwork is perhaps one of the most valued gifts a girl can give, and well worth practising.

mouth music *Normal genital odor is important for both partners, he may react strongly without realizing it*

b i t e s

entle nibbling is part of the general excitatory repertoire. Hard bites at the moment of orgasm excite some people, but for most, like other painful stimuli, they are a turn-off. Women tend to bite more often than men, perhaps because they enjoy being bitten more than men do. Love-bruises, on the neck and elsewhere aren't made by biting but by strong, continuous suction kisses. Sharp nips to the skin aren't as a rule erotic. Be careful of biting at or near orgasm – the jaws go into spasm and you can bite really hard – in fact don't have an orgasm deliberately with a breast, penis or finger in your mouth. The need to bite can be taken out on something neutral like cloth or hair. This seems to be the case where the mammalian program of reflexes is over-tough for human enjoyment.

bites *Hard biting turns most people off, but gentle nibbling is a powerful excitant*

51

c l o t h e d   i n t e r c o u r s e

Really a heavy-petting technique: she keeps her panties
on, he carries out all the movements of straight intercourse
as far as the cloth will allow. Favourite ethnologic variant, for
premarital intercourse – called *badana* in Turkey, *metsha* in
Xhosa, etc. Odd we have no special word.

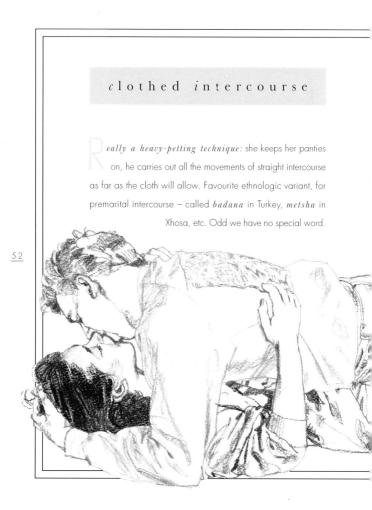

ot reliable as a contraceptive unless the ejaculation position is fully interfemoral, ie with the glans well clear of the vulva, cloth or no cloth. Some people who used this before marriage like to go back to it either as a starter or during menstrual periods. Inclined to be 'dry' and make the man sore if it goes on too long – many women can get a fair orgasm from it.

clothed intercourse *If it's not reliable as a contraceptive method it doesn't fit the needs of safe sex either*

*f*emoral *i*ntercourse

Another dodge, like clothed intercourse, to preserve virginity, avoid pregnancy, etc, in cultures which cared about virginity and had no contraceptives. Comes for us under the heading of substitutes. Used from before or behind, or in any other posture when she can press her thighs together. The penis goes between them, with the shaft between her labia, but the glans well clear of the vagina, and she presses hard. Gives the woman a special set of sensations — sometimes keener than on penetration, so worth trying. One need not be so rigid about technique as were our forefathers, who had to try to keep sperm out of the vulva at any cost. With care this can be done from behind with the glans on the clitoris, with striking results. Good menstrual variant, or for at least a few strokes before you go in.

femoral intercourse *Gives the woman a special set of sensations*

*f*ighting

To need some degree of violence in sex is statistically pretty normal and the way to meet this need is to learn the purposive uses of play. The over-gentle spouse is likely to be blocked about aggression, and non-plussed by a demand 'now try to rape me.' He's been taught not to treat girls like that — if he's excessively over-gentle, he may be sitting on a strong need to do so.

With a normal partner, don't be ashamed if you really fight but don't treat it as a kick, or a way of turning on a partner's aggression. Use play, and keep it in the sexual situation.

Also, as nearly always with man, symbolisms are generally bigger kicks than over-literal enactments. But some couples get a lot of fun out of extended struggles, premeditated or impromptu. Enthusiasts go in for elaborate handicaps: time limits, no-biting and so on, and others play elaborate finding-fault-and-spanking games. Women who dig an extra sensation of violence and/or helplessness differ whether they feel this more held down or tied up: men can take out quite a lot of the violence component in the actual process of penetration and working for orgasm.

Nothing that has been said excludes the tenderness of sex. If you haven't learned that sexual violence can be tender and tenderness violent, you haven't begun to play as real lovers, unless you are people whose tenderness is absolutely unalloyed: these needn't worry about the risks of fighting.

fighting *Mock violence can turn some people on, but avoid treating it as a kick*

exercises *Any new trick*
merits a practice session

exercises

T*he Viennese Turnergesellschaft professor* tried to make
sex into a form of physical training. Good general tone cer-
tainly helps, but it's equally true that sexual exercise tones you up
better than jogging.

Adolescent masturbation, if it's guiltless and enjoyed, is one
of the best specifically sexual exercises, and the man can use it at
any age in learning to slow down his response to a level which
gives the girl a chance. She, for her part, can learn to use her
vaginal and pelvic muscles 'by throwing her mind into the part
concerned,' says Richard Burton. This superlative knack can be
learned, because girls in South India learn it. How exactly they
learn has never been written down unfortunately, and the first
person to teach this properly to women who don't have the knack
naturally will make a fortune. Whether the commercial device
with a rubber cylinder and a pressure-gauge helps we simply
don't know, since our female half has the trick naturally. The

technique to try would involve having a bulb in the vagina and a light or pressure gauge to enable you to know when you were doing the right thing. Anyone can learn to waggle his ears in any direction in 30 minutes flat if he watches the ear on closed-circuit TV. This makes us think that the commercial gadget is worth trying. If she 'throws her mind' with him *in situ* she should master it, and he can tell her when she is succeeding. Once learned it is wholly involuntary and needs no effort.

What we do suggest is that for any new trick you arrange a practice session in anticipation. The time to learn new figures isn't on the ice rink or dance floor. The most common reason that an elaboration you both wanted disappoints, whether it's a fancy posture or some dodge such as bondage which needs to be quickly and efficiently set up, is the attempt to use it in actual, excited lovemaking 'from cold' – so that you mess about, lose the thread, and wish you hadn't bothered with it or blame whoever suggested it. The usual and regrettable outcome is never to try again.

Not that rehearsal need be coldblooded or taken out of actual lovemaking. Anticipation being good in itself, you first fantasize about it, sit down together, plan, and rehearse. Then fit the actual

exercises *If it works first time, go with it!*

61

trial-for-size into the waiting periods between bouts – when you're both excited enough not to feel silly, but not ready to go completely: try it while waiting for the next erection. Remember even James Galway has to practice the flute, though in love once learned is never forgotten. If it works first time you should get the erection – in that case go where it takes you. This means you can rehearse something new for each special occasion, mastering every movement but quite deliberately holding back and not playing it live until the appointed time. The waiting will help when it arrives.

To practice things you must try in full erection, make the effort and try the new posture when you have one – either without movement, if you are set on waiting until later, or switching after a few strokes to something else. Of course, if it takes over, as it may, you might as well carry on, and turn practice into performance there and then. For most postures you can try wearing g-strings, so as to get the motions without actual contact, and some people find this exciting in itself.

exercises *Quite a few women can get an orgasm when riding, especially bareback*

The JOY OF SEX ® Series

Copyright © 1997 by Mitchell Beazley

Published by Crown Publishers, Inc., 201 East 50th Street, New York,
New York 10022. Member of the Crown Publishing Group.

Random House, Inc., New York, Toronto, London, Sydney, Auckland
http://www.randomhouse.com/

CROWN is a trademark of Crown Publishers, Inc.

Printed in Hong Kong

Library of Congress Cataloging-in-Publication Data
is available on request.

ISBN 0-609-60032-X

10 9 8 7 6 5 4 3 2 1

First American Edition

Material in this book excerpted from *The Joy of Sex*

THE Joy OF Sex

sexual foreplay

Alex Comfort, M.B., D.Sc.

Illustrated by
John Raynes

Crown Publishers, Inc., New York

63